Why I VOTE TRUMP and YOU should TOO

By Venera Lyonhart

Phoenix, Arizona

March 25, 2023

About the author

I have been born and raised in Bulgaria which is neighboring country of former Yugoslavia.
Bulgaria and Yugoslavia, both were five centuries under Ottoman Empire slavery. In the span of 500 years Russia fought the Caliphate in 12 wars and the Polish King John III Sobieski defeated the Ottoman Empire army on September 11, 1683 in the battle for Vienna.

Growing up as atheist in a socialist country, I now consider freedom to be the most precious gift from GOD.

Freedom does not mean lawlessness and destruction, but creativity, growth, expansion and thriving unrestricted in time and space.

Saying that, we must protect freedom, fight for it and preserve it for our children and their children.

At this critical times for our nation America needs Trump to take us out of the ditch of destruction and bring us back on the right path to prosperity.
What GOD revealed to me you are not going to believe it.

Venera Lyonhart

Daniel 7:7

"AFTER THAT, IN MY VISION AT NIGHT I LOOKED, AND THERE BEFORE ME WAS A FOURTH BEAST – TERRIFYING AND FRIGHTENING AND VERY POWERFUL. IT HAD LARGE IRON TEETH; IT CRUSHED AND DEVOURED ITS VICTIMS AND TRAMPLED UNDERFOOT WHATEVER WAS LEFT. IT WAS DIFFERENT FROM ALL THE FORMER BEASTS, AND IT HAD TEN HORNS."

Artist
SHOT

$29.45
Plus delivery costs

🛒 BUY NOW

➔ Customize

• • • • •

Get this art on other 102+ products ›

Guillotine Long Sleeve Baby

Artist
SHOT

$21.00
Plus delivery costs

🛒 BUY NOW

➔ Customize

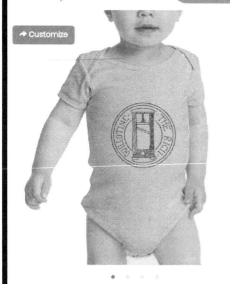

• • • • •

Get this art on other 102+ products ›

Guillotine Baby Bodysuit

★★★★★ + Read & Write Reviews (100)

☰   Search Google Shopping   🛒 ⊚

Guillotine 2020 Onesie | Guillotine

Buying options

About this page ⓘ

$20.00
+$0.00 est. tax
$6.99 delivery

Visit site

☰ cafe press   Search Cafe... 🔍   🛒

< Classic Baby Bodysuits
< Cure For The 1 Percent Infant Bodysuit Baby Light Bodysuit

● ○

Color: Sky Blue

→ Customize

50% OFF

Master Of The Flying Guillotine Baby Bodysuit

KEEP
CALM
AND
FOCUS ON
GUILLOTINE

Color: Sky Blue

Size: Select Size   Size Chart

| 0-3M | 3-6M | 6-12M | 12-18M | 18-24M |

Quantity

− 1 +

~~$24.99~~

$18.74

Teepublic | Guillotine Drop Onesie | Punk
$20.00 from TeePublic
+$5.99 shipping

Teepublic | Guillotine Onesie | Falling Guillotine
$20.00 from TeePublic
+$7.99 shipping

Teepublic | Guillotine 2020 Onesie | Guillotine 2020
$20.00 from TeePublic
+$5.99 shipping

Teepublic | Pretty Guillotine Floral Onesie | Guillotine
$20.00 from TeePublic
+$7.99 shipping

Teepublic | Guillotine 2020 Onesie | Guillotine
$20.00 from TeePublic
+$5.99 shipping

Teepublic | Guillotine Scratch Onesie | Guillotine
$20.00 from TeePublic
+$7.99 shipping

Teepublic | Guillotine II Onesie | Guillotine
$20.00 from TeePublic
+$5.99 shipping

☰ Menu   ⊤ TEEPUBLIC   🛒 Cart

Discover designs just for you   🔍

Guillotine Kids T-Shirt
Guillotine Kids T-Shirt Designed and Sold by valentinahramov

Color: Heather

Visit

Assassin's Creed Unity Mens T-Shirt - Red Blue Trident And Assassin Image...

$18.99* · In stock · Brand: Bioworld

This white 100% cotton tee is perfect for fans of assassins creed., Officially Licensed Product. * It's The Shirt you Always wanted * Official ...

Visit

Assassin's Creed Syndicate - Logo White

$10.49* · In stock · Brand: Tripping Yarns

Assassin's Creed Syndicate logo on a white T shirt.

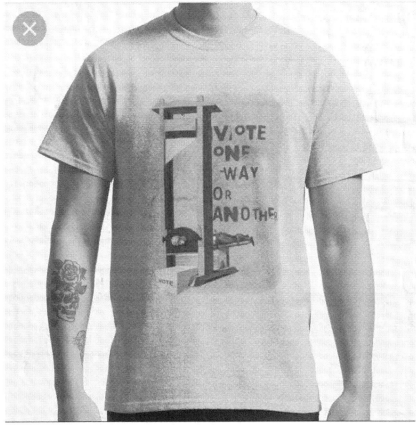

For the original Time Magazine cover go to:

http://YourHillary.US

CAPITOL HILL OCCUPIED PROTEST

JUNE—JULY, 2020

BEHEADED TEACHER IN FRANCE IMAGE MIRRORS THE SEATTLE SIGN

OCTEBER, 2020

Hillary Clinton: Pelosi Ready to Unleash Liberal Hell on America if Biden Wins (VIDEO)

By Jim Hoft
Published October 29, 2020 at 11:15am
881 Comments

Hillary Clinton warned Americans radical Speaker Nancy Pelosi is ready to unleash hell on America if Joe Biden wins the presidential election.

Via **Paul Bedard:**

ies > Men > Men's Clothing > Men's Shirts > Men's T-Shirts

1 of 3

• • •

Guillotines Are Coming | Populist Rage | Adult Unisex Short-Sleeve T-Shirt

 sewmellowdramatic (64 ★)
100% positive feedback

$23.00

Paul Bedard ✔
@SecretsBedard · Follow

Hillary Clinton: Pelosi ready to unleash liberal tsunami after Biden win.

'Now, thankfully Nancy Pelosi bless her heart in every way we can, has teed up a lot of great legislation," Clinton told SiriusXM's Signal Boost this morning.
washex.am/2TvgdiL

8:54 AM · Oct 28, 2020

♡ 26   ⬤ Reply   ⬀ Copy link

Read 40 replies

TRENDING: BREAKING: Bombshell Presentation Reveals Identities Of Maricopa County Elections Employees Who Deleted Files From Election Server BEFORE Maricopa County Audit

Hillary Clinton: You know, I've told the Obama campaign, uh, I mean I told the Biden campaign and the Biden transition that they're going to have to move really fast because let's assume we take back the senate. It matters if we take it back and have 50 votes, or 51 votes or more. And we're going to have to move very quickly. And thankfully. **Nancy Pelosi, and bless her heart in every way we can, has teed up a lot of liberal legislation.** It's been sitting there dying in Mitch McConnell's office. But she has legislated on everything we care about. Even bipartisan legislation. So I would hope that if we get the Democratic Senate... if we want to get something done again. **And one of the areas we'll have to move quickly on is the courts. We're gonna have to move quickly on everything, election reform, climate change, COVID relief, expanding healthcare, everything that we care about.**

The "new page for America" is the history of Europe and the 500 years of Ottoman empire beheading millions of Christians. Copying the Barbarian invasion and the Caliphate's medieval concurring of Europe, Hillary Clinton is planning to overtake the world with radical Islam and Sharia law.

Daily **Mail**   MORE STORIES

Hillary Clinton celebrates a 'new page for America and repudiation of Trump' four years after her crushing defeat as Joe Biden becomes next President - while Bill says former VP 'will bring us all together'

By Jennifer Smith For Dailymail.com
17:55 07 Nov 2020, updated 05:55 08 Nov 2020

The 2016 Hillary Clinton's in burka mural in Australia when she thought she'll be the President of the United States.

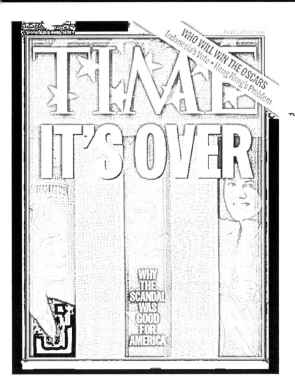

WHO WILL WIN THE OSCARS
Indonesia's Vote • Hong Kong's Problem

TIME
IT'S OVER

WHY THE SCANDAL WAS GOOD FOR AMERICA

AUGUST 12, 2002

NINE MONTHS BEFORE 9/11 the U.S. had a bold plan to attack al-Qaeda. It wasn't carried out until the towers fell

TIME

SPECIAL REPORT

The Secret History

TIME

SPECIAL · REPORT

WHILE AMERICA SLEPT

WHAT BUSH KNEW BEFORE 9/11
WHY SO LITTLE WAS DONE
HOW THE SYSTEM IS STILL BROKEN

INSIDE TIPS ON ORGANIC GROWING

HIGH TIMES

UP IN SMOKE
Bill Clinton Goes to Pot

LOUIS ARMSTRONG ORIGINAL REEFER MAN

JESSE THE BODY VENTURA FIGHTS FOR HEMP

SENSI IN SEATTLE

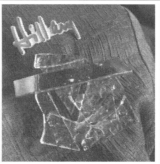

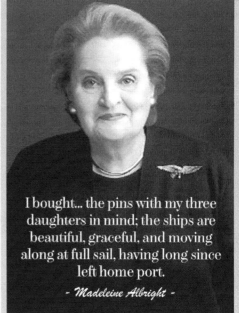

I bought... the pins with my three daughters in mind; the ships are beautiful, graceful, and moving along at full sail, having long since left home port.

- Madeleine Albright -

READ MY PINS

STORIES FROM A DIPLOMAT'S JEWEL BOX

MADELEINE ALBRIGHT

Watch live:
Hillary
in Denver

Wednesday
August 3, 2016
Tune in on Facebook!

Hillary

PLANET HILLARY

Details about Rare Vintage 90s BILL
CLINTON "Will Work For Head" Shirt...
$149.99* · In stock · Brand: Fruit of the Loom
Rare Vintage 90s BILL CLINTON "Will Work For Head" Shirt Political
Sexual Humor. Shipped with USPS First Class., 🔥INSTAGRAM ...

Visit

THE
CLINTONS
THEIR STORY IN PHOTOGRAPHS

Created by NEW YORK TIMES
Bestselling Author/Editor
DAVID ELLIOT COHEN

Foreword by
CHRIS MATTHEWS

YourHillary.US

FREE PDF DOWNLOAD
PHOTOS ONLY FILES

TOWN & COUNTRY

BILL CLINTON

ARKANSAS TIMES

HILLARY CLINTON

Newsweek

Exclusive: Excerpts
From Hillary Rodham Clinton's
New Book—And a Candid Interview
on the White House Scandals

Saint or Sinner?

Watch live: Hillary in Denver
Wednesday August 3, 2016
Tune in on Facebook!

Hillary

VS

Senate Committee to Investigate the
JANUARY 6TH
Attack on the United States Capital

Movie Mania   **Angels & Demons   2009**

Pope Benedict XVI

December 31, 2022

Google it

PRICE $4.50

THE
NEW YORKER

JULY 21, 2008

NEW GLARUS
CLINTON ODER TRUMP
So leben und wählen die
Schweizer Auswanderer

HELLS ANGELS
DER ROCKER-GIPFEL
Die Exklusiv-Reportage
vom Geheimtreffen!

MICHELLE &
BARACK OBAMA

Simply
the Best!

Wir vermissen euch schon jetzt

Becoming

NETFLIX | MAY 6

Newsweek

THE OBAMA CONQUEST
Lucky General or Master of the Game?
BY DANIEL KLAIDMAN

BY David Frum

PLUS:
BY MICHAEL TOMASKY
BY MICHELLE GOLDBERG
AND 2012 WINS & FAILS,
MICHELLE VS. ANN

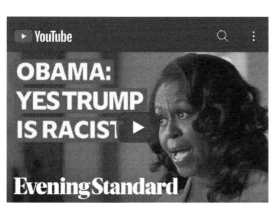

▶ YouTube

OBAMA:
YES TRUMP
IS RACIST ▶

Evening Standard

Michelle Obama calls Trump 'racist' while
appealing to white working-class Americans
12K views · 1 year ago

SPECIAL STATE OF THE UNION
the Atlantic
How The New York Times Could Survive
Michelle Obama in Black and White
Football's Hardest Job
THE END OF WHITE AMERICA?

12. **She was the first female partner at her law firm in Arkansas.** She worked for the Rose Law Firm from 1977 to 1993.

Ph

Guillotine Ballot Box Classic T-shirt |
Redbubble Vote Classic Tee

$22.66 · In stock

Visit

2022 Elections Guillotine Unisex T-Shirt
by Bella + Canvas White / S

🔖
SAVE

Buying options

About these results ⓘ

$27.95
+$2.40 est. tax
Free delivery by Fri, Dec 23

printgravy

Visit site

I have the most wonderful news!

Jesus Christ was conceived by

The Holy Spirit and

The Holy Spirit is a Sound!

The Sound of the Word of God!

I would like everybody to know that

Jesus was drawn with the Sound of

The Father's Love!

Jesus is alive and he is authentic!

God is always good, and He loved the world so much
That He sacrificed His only son to save us.

Jesus came to bridge our separation from God.

When Jesus left Israel to be with the Father,

God sent the Holy Spirit to teach us all things and be

Our FOREVER Helper and Counselor.

And the Spirit of GOD

was hovering over the

face of the waters

Genesis 1:2

In the beginning was

The Word, and the Word

was with GOD and the

Word was GOD

John 1:1

Hold fast the pattern of

sound words which You

have heard from me, in faith

and love which are in

Christ Jesus.

2 Timothy 1:13

NKJ version

The LORD did not set His love on you nor choose you because you were more in number than any other people, for you were the least of all peoples;

Deuteronomy 7:7

* On Sept. 11, 1565 ENDED the Ottoman empire's
Great siege of Malta
* Sept. 11, 1609 King Philip II announced
The Expulsion of Muslims from Spain
* Sept. 11, 1609 The Island of Manhattan was
Discovered by Henry Hudson
* 2001 Months later on July 4, 1776 America was founded
* Sept. 11, 1683 ENDED the Ottoman empire
Siege of Vienna
* Sept. 11, 1697 The Battle of Zenta (Senta, Serbia)
* Sept. 11, 2001 BEGAN a new WAR on our Civilization

The painting Baptism of Christ
by Arent de Gelder from 1710

Is in the Fitzwilliam Museum in London.

Arent de Gelder was a student of Rembrandt

Ye shall know them by their fruits

Matthew 7:16

Ye shall know them by their fruits

Matthew 7:16

DEMOCRATS ARE DONE, THE RED WAVE IS BACK, TRUMP IS COMING

Text SAVE to 88022

TEXT FREEDOM TO 512345

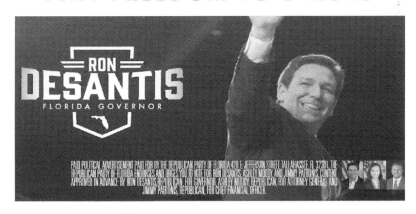

FREEDOM IS HERE
TO STAY

Remarks Prepared by President Donald J. Trump

I want to take this moment to THANK YOU for all of the support you've given our movement.

When our America First movement began eight years ago, everyone in the media and the establishment said we were doomed to fail.

But YOU proved the entire world wrong.

You showed the world that America can still be a nation *of*, *for*, and *by* the people.

Patriots like YOU are the source of my courage, my resolve, and my hope.

There's not a single doubt in my mind that we will prevail, win back the White House, and Make America Great Again!

I am confident that America's greatest days lie ahead!

Made in United States
Troutdale, OR
10/05/2024

23438198R00020